WHAT YOU LEAVE *BEHIND*

NICK POURGOURIDES

WHAT YOU LEAVE *BEHIND*

A short family memoir

Nick Pourgourides

First published in 2022

Copyright © 2022 Nick Pourgourides

The author has partnered with
Variety, the Children's Charity to donate 100% of the proceeds of this book to help raise funds for disabled and disadvantaged children across the UK
www.variety.org.uk

WHAT YOU LEAVE *BEHIND*

Born in London in 1978, Nick Pourgourides has worked in entertainment publicity for the past two decades. He began his published writing career with 'More, Please,' a biography of the late actor Kenneth More. The book featured in the Amazon best seller list upon publication and was covered in national media including BBC Radio 4, The Bookseller, Daily Mail, The Daily Telegraph and The Stage. He has also written for national weeklies including The Lady and The Oldie.

'What You Leave Behind,' a short family memoir is his second published book.

He lives in South-West London with his wife Rebecca and pet Cockapoo Clementine.

Rebecca and Clementine, you make it all
worthwhile

For my mother, whose indomitable spirit is
my guiding light

In memory of my grandparents

A portrait of my grandfather, taken in 1911 at
Chinese Maritime Customs

1

GUANIXI

My greatest wish was to have had one conversation alone with my grandfather. Just the two of us. I have so many questions to ask him. My mother has often told me of the uncanny resemblance I bear to him. The similarities in our personalities. Our outlook on life and even our sense of style. Having died long before I was born, our meeting was an impossibility. He has remained an almost mythical character in our family with only my mother to act as the narrator of his story. To her, as with all daughters whose beloved father have passed on, he was held up as a great paragon of virtue. It was that image that held my curiosity as a child. I knew extraordinarily little about the actual man.

My grandmother was still very much alive whilst I was growing up, but she was an elusive figure, emotionally inaccessible in so many ways. Kindness was always conveyed at arm's length. To this day, when I close my eyes, I can still picture her in our family home at Christmas during the 1980s.

The scent of Pears soap which seemed to follow her around wherever she went. The fresh tissue she always carried under the right sleeve arm of her cardigan. Her immaculate but conservative attire from the stalwart of British clothing brands, Eastex. Her penchant for a daily dose of the vitamin B supplement, Brewer's Yeast. My grandmother was quintessentially English. I remember how she would sit on our sofa and read The Times newspaper, occasionally watching television when the likes of 'Dad's Army' or the evening news came on. Her home at 28 Ashenden Close, Canterbury, was a small but modest abode that was simple in decor aside for a luxurious, thickly piled red carpet in the corridor, which my little feet would always sink into. The welcome I received was unfortunately just as remote as it had been at Christmas. Each time I visited I would be ushered into the living room to sit on the rather uncomfortable moquette sofa to take 'afternoon tea,' before being left with no illusion that the remainder of the stay was for my grandmother to spend time alone with her daughter. I was expected to go out, as were my two older brothers and my father. There was little of her own life's story that she shared whilst I was growing up, and I do not recall her ever mentioning my grandfather.

I remember how strange I thought it was that there were no family photographs on display in her house. I only had my mother's memories of my grandfather to call upon and even those were rather limited. He had died when she was eighteen years old. What I did learn was that he was five feet tall and had short brown hair and green eyes. He was extremely loving to his family, and kind and generous to those he knew. The opposite of how I saw my grandmother. He was also smartly dressed and always conducted himself as the perfect gentleman. His favourite colour was taupe green. He had a love for the Irish tenor John McCormack, who sang such classic Gaelic songs as 'The Long Road to Tipperary,' and 'Danny Boy' (Londonderry Air)'. His favourite tipple was Irish whiskey. My grandfather was also well read, taking a particular interest in history, especially books about the American West, a period that had only recently passed in his lifetime.

On my wedding day in 2015, my mother presented me with his solid gold J.W. Benson wristwatch. A highly respected London watchmakers during the second half of the 19th Century. This had been my grandmother's wedding gift to him when they married in the 1930s. It is one of only a handful of personal items that he owned which survives to this day. The rest include an album of family photographs, a silver topped Malacca wooden walking cane (which my mother later presented to me on my 40th birthday), and a heavy black steamer trunk from the London-based E.J. Pearson and Sons, a world-renowned maker of leather goods. The trunk, from their Victor line, also bears my grandfather's name in heavy white paint.

Whilst I was writing this book, I suddenly had a flashback to a tarot reading I once had in the late 1990s. I remember how I had entered the experience purely out of a curiosity to discover what attracted so many people to have their fortune told. Before the session had even started, the tarot reader told me that she could see someone standing behind me. I turned around and laughed. "Ha, ha. Who?" She wagged her finger in disapproval and gestured upward. "Not there, silly. I meant in spirit. I do not know who they are by name!" She then focused her eyes on the large, pictured cards in front of her which she had spread across a black satin tablecloth. I watched on with some amusement. "I get the feeling that whoever it is they are somewhat patriarchal toward you." She then closed her eyes and paused for a moment before resuming: "I can see clearer now. It is a male figure. Older. He is friendly but reserved. You appear drawn to grandfatherly figures, don't you?" There was certainly truth in this. I have always tended to gravitate towards them because I had no relationship with my own, my father's having also died. The reader continued to run her hands over the cards before concluding our meeting. "Whoever it is, he seems to be keeping a caring, watchful eye over you." I must admit that I did not think much of the experience at the time and soon forgot about it. It was strange how this memory had suddenly popped back into my head after all these years. Did this figure mean something after all? Was that my mother's father?

As time went on, I tried on many occasions to research his life through the usual records of public libraries and ancestral websites, but always with limited success. Because of this, there was little I was able to do to have his name remembered in any meaningful way. Something I have always been determined to do. The Chinese call this 'Guanxi' (关系), loosely meaning to have a strong relationship with someone, which can involve a moral obligation. The term perfectly suited the connection I had toward my grandfather.

Two years ago, and purely by chance some previously unseen family records were unearthed by my mother. The discovery of which felt as if a securely locked door to the past had finally been picked. One doorway led to another and before long I was finally able to piece together enough of his life to be able to retell it here.

It was whilst researching my grandfather's history that a personal, life-changing experience occurred that forced me to confront my own feelings regarding self-acceptance and family legacy. In many ways, they were so inextricably linked to this book's overarching theme of ancestral continuity that it seemed appropriate to bookend them here in the final chapter of this short family memoir.

2

SHANGHAILANDER

My grandfather was born Patrick Joseph Gleeson in Limerick on 20th November 1885. The same year that the writer D.H. Lawrence and the fashion designer Hugo Boss are born. Queen Victoria is on the throne. The motorcycle is invented, and the writer Mark Twain publishes the classic literary children's story 'The Adventures of Huckleberry Finn.'

Patrick is the middle child of seven siblings to mother and housewife Mary, and father Daniel Gleeson, a local pig buyer. Both staunch Irish Catholics from humble origins, they married in Limerick in 1879. Of their children, it would be Patrick who would have his eyes firmly set on a life far beyond the west of Ireland.

My grandfather had not been able to attend university due to the expensive schooling fees. What had come out of a lack of formal education was a relentless drive from within to better himself. Something that I have also inherited. This unwavering determination compelled him to travel further than any of his family would ever do, to a place that would bring him success, love, and a great deal of loss and suffering.

In his early twenties, Patrick travelled to the London office of Imperial Maritime Customs Service at 26 Old Queen Street in Westminster, who were seeking young men to join the Service in China. Founded in 1854, Imperial Maritime Customs was a tax collection agency that, although under Chinese governmental control, was uniquely administered by foreign staff. It was set up following the Taiping Rebellion, China's civil war which saw the country's ports without the means to collect revenue, several of which were open to foreign trade. Despite a quarter of the staff being British, half of those employed were Chinese. The rest were made up of Americans, French, German, Italians, Japanese, Norwegians, and Russians. Later renamed Chinese Maritime Customs, the Service functioned as a crucial organisation tasked not only with customs excise, but also the management of trade and commerce between China and the rest of the world. It also patrolled the country's territorial waters before China had formed its own navy, as well as handling weather charting and postal management.

After successfully completing the interview and examination process in 1911, Patrick boarded the first of several steamships on the six-week long voyage to Shanghai. He must have been filled with a mixture of emotions as to what life would hold for him in such a far-off land. I like to imagine that he might even have taken comfort in the Irish proverb 'He who travels has stories to tell.'

Upon arrival, Patrick would have walked down the jetty into Shanghai's hot and humid air, where he would have been greeted with a view of The Bund (China's riverfront) and its key landmarks, including Custom House. Rebuilt several times, the building as it stands today was designed by British architects Palmer and Turner, who were also responsible for many other structures on The Bund, including the Municipal Government Building and the Cathay Hotel. At the time of its construction in 1927, Custom House was the tallest building standing at 91 meters. An impressive fascia designed in the neo-classical style, featuring Doric columns at its entrance and an impressive clock tower above fashioned after London's Big

Ben. Patrick officially started working for the Service on 1st March as a Watcher, charged with tallying foreign goods arriving in harbour.

At this point in history, Shanghai and Hankow were two of five ports in China partially divided into independent Western settlements, a result of the British victory in the first war on Opium which took place between 1839–1842. The Treaty of Nanking had allowed these ports to be opened to foreign traders, and thus international territories were formed by the British, French, and Americans. The 1844 Anglo-Chinese Treaty of the Bogue then gave its inhabitants diplomatic security and exemption from local Chinese law. By 1863, the Americans had joined the British to create The International Settlement. Here a bubble of Western civilisation was formed in East Asia out of the image of their ancestral lands, from shops to bars, restaurants, and even cinemas. Although not a British colony, this was still very much a product of imperialism and as a result its place in history sits very uncomfortably in the mind to this day.

Unlike other ports, Shanghai was especially cosmopolitan, a crowded metropolis made up of Chinese and foreign citizens, known as

'Shanghailanders.' Shanghai was considered a melting pot of decadence and extravagance by Eastern standards, with taxis and trams, as well as buildings and walkways lit with the newest invention of the time, electricity. The most luxurious hotels were fully equipped with lifts, hot water, and heating. The Astor House Hotel positioned itself as the 'Waldorf Astoria of the Orient,' with such extravagance as a 500-seat dining room and dance floor. The Cathay Hotel had opulently decorated interiors adorned with Lalique crystal. Then there was the chic gentleman's Shanghai Club, infamous for housing the world's longest bar standing at 34-metres in an L-shaped configuration and built from solid mahogany. This was the focal point of social activity for the 'Taipans,' the foreign-born senior business executives working in China. It is most likely my grandfather would have spent a great deal of time here. The celebrated playwright Noël Coward arrived in 1930 and wrote that he could see the curvature of the earth as he lay his cheek on the Long Bar. One of his seminal works, 'Private Lives,' is believed to have been written in Shanghai, with the final draft completed at the Cathay Hotel.

Throughout the 1920s and into the 1930s, the wealthy and the famous would visit Shanghai in their droves, including actors Charlie Chaplin, Douglas Fairbanks, Mary Pickford, and the playwright Eugene O'Neill. Shanghai also possessed a vibrant and exotic nightlife. Everything could be found here, from jazz and cabaret nightclubs, to gambling dens, opium bars, and brothel houses, all awash with locals, sailors and tourists sampling the city's nightlife. Shanghai must have been overwhelming to the senses for a young Irish Catholic from a humble background. What my grandfather made of it, or indeed how much he immersed himself in its charms is open to question, but based on what is known of his character, I can easily imagine him taking a reserved and cautious approach.

Since joining the Service, Patrick's career had progressed quickly. From 1912 until 1915, he worked as a Tidewaiter, with authority to inspect ships cargo to ensure that custom regulations were being adhered to. Service staff would often move between ports when needed and from 1916 until 1918, Patrick was seconded to Tiensin. He would move back to Shanghai between 1919 and 1920 to take up a position as an Assistant Examiner, tasked with scrutinising the value and rate of customs duty declared on goods. 1921 saw a year's attachment to the port of Mengtze, before returning once again to Shanghai in 1922.

The late 1920s would see Patrick promoted to the role of Acting Appraiser, where he learned every facet of the business of verifying whether the goods imported were the same which the importers had declared in their shipping documents. 1931-1934 were spent working out of the port of Canton in the same role. He returned to Shanghai in 1935 to assume the position of an Appraiser. He was now a successfully civil servant and about to meet the love of his life, my grandmother.

Born Mary (May) Lillian Julia Pearce in Mile End, London on 23rd January 1898, my grandmother was daughter to mother Rachel, who suffered with heart disease, and Albert William James Pearce (who died of pneumonia when she was eighteen months old). My grandmother would have a tumultuous upbringing being passed from relative to relative. She had two sisters, a twin called Agnes who was brought up by another cousin, and an elder half-sister called Florrie, who lived with another relative. Neither saw much of each other.

At the age of fourteen, my grandmother started her first job working in a blind home for young wounded soldiers who had recently returned from the front at the start of The Great War. Three years later, she fell in love for the very first time with one of the injured, who sadly died not that long after. It no doubt had a significant impact on her. Mary's desire to care for invalids led her to eventually train as a nurse at St. Olave's Hospital in Rotherhithe. She completed her teaching in 1923 at the age of twenty-five. Upon graduation, Mary was singled out by Lady Du Maurier, the head of the colonial medical service. Du Maurier saw the makings of a great nurse and encouraged my grandmother to join Crown Agents, Britain's overseas non-profit development company which helped to improve health systems in developing countries. In 1931, Mary's first posting was at a hospital in Nicosia, Cyprus. A year later she moved to Shanghai at the age of thirty-four. It was whilst working here at the International Hospital that she met a Franciscan priest who would introduce her to my grandfather. The attraction was instant. They courted, eventually marrying on 16th October 1935 at a Catholic church in Shanghai. The event even made it into the most influential foreign newspaper of its time, the North China

Daily News. Their wedding portrait is illustrated in the newspaper's magazine supplement. They would spend three years in Shanghai before moving to the port of Hankow, where Patrick had been reassigned to carry out his Custom duties. Hankow was (and still is as part of modern-day Wuhan), a key transportation hub for China due to its position north of the Han and Yangtze Rivers.

As part of my grandfather's position, he was given residence at St. John's Vicarage in Hankow. A large, two-storey property which accommodated the local clergy as well as other British diplomats and their families. The Vicarage also included the use of servants and a chauffeur. Here they led an idyllic but simple life in relative comfort. My mother would later tell me how he had learned Mandarin and Chinese during this period, as well as being taught how to cook authentic Chinese food, something he would continue to do even in his later years. China had and would have the single greatest impact on his life.

During this period, my grandparents quickly integrated themselves into society. They first became members of The Hankow Club, an important social establishment for foreign residents whose facilities included a bowling alley, card room, five billiard tables, a bar and restaurant.

It was here that my grandparents were introduced to one of the Club's staff, Sheila Kathleen Mary Butterfield, and her husband, Henry Samuel Butterfield. A stockbroker by trade, Henry's family owned the well-known trading company Butterfield & Swire, which dealt in British imports as well as insurance and shipping. Butterfield & Swire's headquarters was located next to Custom House, and as a result Henry's work would often overlap with that of my grandfather's. Over time, both couples became close friends with one another.

The Hankow Race Club and Recreation Ground was also another venue my grandparents frequented. A popular retreat for foreign residents that contained a swimming pool, a clay pigeon shooting range, a bowling green, football and cricket fields, twelve tennis courts, and even two golf courses.

Patrick became involved with the British Consul during this period, which also resulted in a further elevation in his social standing. Although not part of the elite, he was introduced to many, high-profile dignitaries including the leader of the

Republic of China, Generalissimo Chiang Kai-shek, and the First Lady, Madame Chiang Kai-shek. My grandparents would also travel for business and pleasure. One trip in November 1936 saw them onboard the RMS Queen Mary, which only three months earlier had seen the gigantic steamer awarded the Blue Ribbon for the fastest Atlantic crossing by an ocean liner. They would also holiday in Pompeii, marvelling at the vast archaeological site in southern Italy, as well as venturing to Yokohama to visit the hot sulphur springs at Mount Unzen, which only two years earlier had been chosen as Japan's first national park.

My grandparents wedding portrait taken in Shanghai on
16th October 1935. The event even made it into the
North China Daily News

3

LOST AND FOUND

By 1941, my grandfather had reached the high-ranking position of Chief Appraiser and was continuing to excel in his work life. In private, there was great sadness ahead. My grandparents had tried for children as early as 1940, first conceiving a son named John, who was sadly born a stillbirth. At the time, the quality of healthcare in China was poor for women facing childbirth, but Maritime Customs took diligent care of its employees and their spouses, making sure they had access to the best medical treatment that was available, despite its shortcomings.

Their second child, daughter Mary Patricia, was successfully delivered on 16th February 1940. The eminent Catholic priest Edward J. Galvin had become acquainted with my grandparents and accepted the offer of being made Mary Patricia's godfather. Galvin had led the first Irish missionaries to China and was the first Bishop of Hanyang. For a few months, my grandparents were full of the joys of life as new parents.

Heartbreakingly, Mary Patricia's health would soon decline, and she passed away a mere five and half months later at the International Hospital on 1st of August 1940. She was buried at the New International Cemetery, Hankow. Upsettingly, this sacred burial ground has long since disappeared.

Joy for my grandparents finally arrived on 6th September 1941 when my mother, Christine Mary was born at the International Hospital and survived. She was baptised at the hospital's chapel on 20th September in the presence of her godparents, Henry and Sheila Butterfield. Life had finally given my grandparents the chance at raising a child. My mother has often told me how protective her parents were of her when she was growing up because of what had happened to her earlier siblings. Even the slightest cold would see my mother whisked off to bed and the doctor called. It is easy to understand why.

For now, life for the family was blissful. My mother recently told me an endearing story that her parents had shared when she was growing up. Each morning before work, the breakfast table would be laid out in the garden of the Vicarage. As soon as my grandfather had taken his seat, an old hen would appear and make its way over to the table, expecting its own breakfast to be served. My grandparents grew fond of it, eventually naming it Biddy. A common Irish diminutive for the name Bridget, meaning 'strength or exalted one.' Since the 18th century, Biddy was used as a slang term for an old or fussy woman. Given the hen's nature, it is likely the former was the reasoning behind the choice in name.

A photograph of my grandparents and their new-born
daughter Mary Patricia taken in Hankow in 1940

4

THE LORD GIVETH AND THE LORD TAKETH AWAY
(JOB 1:21)

The Second World War would come to China in August 1937 following the full Japanese occupation of the country's cities, including Hankow and Shanghai. Despite this, the Japanese army stopped short of advancing on the International and Foreign Settlements because of their extraterritoriality. With the Japanese bombing of Pearl Harbor marking the official declaration of war against the West, the final invasion was swift. To begin with, life continued throughout the occupation. Allied citizens were ordered to wear identity armbands, but many continued to work including my grandfather. As time passed and the situation deteriorated, all citizens were first placed under house arrest before being interned in concentration camps, known as Civil Assembly Centres (CAMs).

The family's darkest days came in February 1943, when they were moved from their home to an internment camp at 404 Yu Yuen Road. My mother was only a year old when they arrived. The camp was on the premises of the Western District Public School and the Shanghai Public School for Girls. Yu Yuen Road held over nine hundred internees including many like my grandfather who were employees of Maritime Customs. Prisoners lived in squalid conditions and were fed on a diet of rice and cracked wheat. Although Red Cross parcels were dropped monthly, the Japanese soldiers would often store these away in warehouses to gather dust.

Like many male prisoners interned, the Japanese soldiers tortured my grandfather. It is unclear whether this took place in the camp or at the infamous Bridge House, an old Chinese hotel where many prisoners suffered abhorrent abuse at the hands of their captives. He was once a kind, warm-hearted and generous man, but his suffering at the hands of the Japanese army did much to age him. His hair turned almost completely white overnight.

In April 1943 whilst in Yu Yen Road, my grandparents were reunited with their friends, Henry and Sheila Butterfield and their three children. They stayed close together in the camp for several months before Sheila became extremely ill. Malnutrition was widespread and parents often went without the little food that was available to feed their children. Disease would spread easily striking down many in their prime. Tragically, on 5th October 1943, Sheila passed away at the tender age of thirty-two, most likely of dysentery. Her husband and children would survive. For the next two years, those interned did their best to try and create some form of society within their hellish environment. Everything from recitals to stage plays were performed, alongside the schooling of children. Anything the internees could do to keep their spirits up and add some sense of normality to deal with the horror they had to endure.

By April 1945, bombing raids had hit Yu Yen Road and the remaining prisoners were moved to Yangtzepoo camp, situated in the Sacred Heart Hospital. The environment here was just as dire, with poor sanitary conditions and wide-spread rat infestation. Regular interrogation and beatings became almost a normal sight, and my grandfather was once again subject to abuse. He suffered two broken legs and a stomach haemorrhage during such episodes. My mother is not sure how she remembers this, but on several occasions, prisoners would be woken in the middle of the night and forced to queue up to be counted. Perhaps to see how many were still alive. My grandparents would tell her to bow her head and never look up at the soldier in-charge. Any act that could be taken as belligerence would mean immediate punishment, even for children.

It is incomprehensible to imagine how they all managed. Daily life as a prisoner of war must have seemed like just one big waiting game with only questions to continually ponder over: would they be able to hang on to life long enough to see out the end of the war, and if they did survive what would happen to them? Would they ever be free? It is in these sorts of harrowing moments, which have been consigned to history books, that we in the present have the luxury of asking ourselves, how would we have reacted to such a situation? Do these life and death experiences represent the ultimate test of character?

The war did finally end, and Japan surrendered with the Americans arriving to liberate the camps. The relief at suddenly being set free must have felt like a euphoric tidal wave of exhaustion and disorientation. Would the world they had known still exist? The International Settlement certainly would not. Upon release, my grandmother and mother were but skin and bones, and my grandfather was far too savagely beaten to be able to walk. They were quickly moved into make-shift intensive care units.

As time passed, my grandparents had to decide upon their future. They did not want to stay on in China, and even if they had, the lives they had once known had long since disappeared. Henry Butterfield and the children also decided to repatriate. In November 1945, the family were transported to Hong Kong to board the Bibby Line cargo ship, the Oxfordshire. The ship had been requisitioned by the British Government and converted into a hospital ship for the transfer of British subjects back to England. My grandfather was now aged sixty and saw out the voyage in the ship's sickbay. My grandmother now aged forty-seven, and my mother aged four, were both suffering with Osteomalacia, a softening of their limbs from malnutrition which made it difficult to walk.

My grandparents, my mother, and Uncle Mick in 1946.
The suffering my grandparents had endured during
their internment is plainly visible

5

FULL CIRCLE

Patrick and Mary were now changed people. What must have been going through their minds as they returned to England? China had given them employment and a home, and most importantly a family. England must have represented a regression in their lives. They were incredibly proud people and now they were forced to return with nothing but the physical and emotional scars of war. All they had achieved had been stripped from them. Despite this, they had the fortune of having survived internment, many did not.

The family eventually arrived at Liverpool dock on December 5th, 1945. A long journey by train to Paddington would follow before onward travel to Chase Farm Hospital in Enfield, where they started their long road to recovery. My grandmother's sister, Agnes, lived in Enfield with her husband Harry Griffin and upon the family's discharge from hospital they were invited to stay. This went a long way to help both sisters become reacquainted with one another, and they would stay in regular contact throughout their lives.

When they were strong enough to think about their future, my grandfather took the decision to move the family to Ireland to reconnect with his own relatives for support. My mother told me how her Uncle Mick and Aunty Billie in Limerick were waiting to take them in the moment they arrived. Now began another lengthy process of waiting, this time for the British and Irish governments to process the family resettlement fees. Their small annuity eventually came through in the 1950s, enabling them to rebuild their lives in a new home at number No. 4, Davitt Road in Bray, which they named 'Ladyville.' Here they tried their best to put the past behind them, with varying degrees of success. They never once spoke of their former lives or the hardship they had endured.

It has often been said that this was motivated by the belief in the idiom of a British stiff upper lip. One did not complain, they just got on with things. However, I have come to believe that sharing their experiences, whether they be extreme hardship or loss, would be considered by many to be improper and self-serving, as a whole generation around the world had been affected by war. One family's story would be considered no greater than the next.

To help pay the bills at this time, my grandparents would often take in lodgers. Their lives were basic. In summer, there would be one suit for my grandfather, and a dress each for my grandmother and mother. Winter would bring a second outfit for each. Whatever small savings they managed to scrape together were used to help my mother's education. They also managed to negotiate reduced fees with the Mother Superior at Loreto Convent, where my mother went from the age of eleven, and was a boarder between fourteen and eighteen. By September 1959, my mother had finished school and followed in Mary's footsteps by starting nursing training. She moved to London to join the Royal Northern Hospital in Holloway.

Since 1958, Patrick had been suffering from Angina, most likely a result of his treatment at the hands of the Japanese soldiers. Two years later, on 1st of October 1960, he suffered a major heart attack whilst escorting my mother to Dublin airport to resume her nursing training in London. He was rushed to the Mater Hospital where attempted resuscitation was performed for six minutes. He passed away of Coronary Thrombosis at seventy-four years old. Heartbroken, the family ploughed their grief into organising his church service, which was held at The Holy Redeemer Catholic Church in Bray. He was buried in Saint Peter's Cemetery. His headstone is engraved with an excerpt from Revelations 21:4: 'And there shall be great understanding, no more sorrow, no more pain.' Words that perfectly capture his wartime experiences and ultimate passing.

Despite everything they had been through, my grandparents had achieved their aim of successfully raising a child of their own. When I look at my mother now, I see all the battles they had overcome to give her the best start in life. Had they not survived the war I would not be here today writing this book.

6

LEGACY

"Children should be seen and not heard." The only words I ever remember my grandmother saying to me, and they stuck with me throughout my life. Why? Because they were dismissive? Or that they stood for a desire to keep a child in their place? Neither, to me it reflected the coldness I felt from our limited relationship. Either way I was never able to truly connect with her. She would live to the grand old age of ninety-seven, passing away in her sleep at home on 4th Dec 1995.

During the research and writing of this book, I have been blessed with the opportunity to accurately reflect on those early memories of my grandmother and how they were tainted by the naivety of youth and a lack of understanding of what she had gone through in her life. Perhaps if I had been older when she had been alive and had known what I do now about her life, things might have been different. That wish to have had one conversation alone with my grandfather now extends to my grandmother. I recently discovered a photograph of us together on our own. I am but a baby, but she holds me with such tenderness and love. How wrong I was.

I believe we all experience moments in our lives, good or bad, that alter us. From that point onwards we are changed irrevocably. For me that experience came only a few years ago when my wife, Rebecca and I lost our first child and later found out we were unable to have further children of our own. In my solitude, I often wonder what sort of person he or she would have become. Would they have shared a desire to better themselves that I have had the fortune of inheriting from my grandfather? Poignantly, that question will remain unanswered.

In the fall of 2021, a shaft of light cut through the darkness when Rebecca and I welcomed a puppy cockapoo into our lives. We called her Clementine, the name we had chosen for our daughter if we had been fortunate enough to have had a child of our own. The arrival of our four-legged friend went a long way to re-direct the maternal love we had both been carrying. In fact, it did more than that, it opened our eyes to a whole new world. Being a parent to a puppy has some small echoes of what it must feel like to care for a child of your own: the teething troubles, the tantrums, and the sleepless nights. You are also welcomed into a special club of fellow doggy parents, enabling you a rare and wonderful opportunity to communicate on a level with strangers that breaks with the social norm. You end up making friends very easily as a result, even getting to know neighbours you never knew you had. The whole experience is special and life changing. Clementine has enriched our lives, providing us with unconditional love and finally a family unit of our own. I call her my 'doggie daughter.' Sometimes that is mocked by people who hear it, even friends. I do not care. She's all that we have in our lives. Sometimes, I wonder if I am not just trying to act out a sense of what fatherhood would have been for myself. The rehearsal on endless repeat. We are yet to come to terms with the fact that Clementine will not always be here with us. That is one step too far for us to consider at this point.

There are always moments when being 'childless by involuntary circumstance' as it is called, will hit you. A friend suddenly tells you they are pregnant, or posts on social media about their child's first steps, or first day at school. Life events that remind you of what you do not and will not have. Then there are powerful feelings that take you completely off guard. Feelings of grief, frustration, isolation, yearning, sadness, and yes, even jealousy…

Once I saw a father in the park assembling his son's first kite. The excitement on the child's face was palpable. Suddenly, the kite soared into the blue sky as the father quickly and confidently began to teach his child how to manage it. There he was passing on his own knowledge and his experience with love and care. It struck me. This is how we find immortality. We pass on what we learn to our next generation. What do you do when life has not gifted you with this privilege? From afar I sat on a bench and watched them both with Clementine. She was unaware of what I was thinking. Then came a sudden and intense emotion that was all-consuming. I realised I was mourning something that would never happen for myself, and then came the rage, envy and bitterness. How was it that this man was fortunate enough to experience fatherhood where I was not? The obligatory 'why me?' question hanging over me like a dark rain cloud. How incomplete I felt as a human being. Suddenly, the wind picked up again and the kite rose even higher. Clementine and I both watched as it arched across the sun. I turned my head away and pulled my dog close to me for comfort. We were soon on the move, and thankfully leaving the situation behind us.

Moments like this are thankfully not long-lasting. What does remain however are questions such as: how do I reconcile this struggle? How does anyone in my position? Does not having children of my own make me emotionally underdeveloped? Our society constantly subjects us to the notion that until you have had offspring of your own you are somehow not complete as a human being. There also seems to be a stigma associated with the idea of talking about this issue of 'involuntary childlessness,' as it is also known. Especially for men in this situation, who notoriously find it difficult to share their feelings. Perhaps that is why there is little resources on how to heal this invisible pain. This emotional conundrum has pressed upon me the need to confront my own mortality and strikes at the very heart of the question I have wrestled with these last few years: what is worse than dying? Not to have children to care for you in later life, to remember you by, or to carry on your legacy? To be forgotten by the world you once lived in. Almost as if you had never been born at all. My grandfather was lucky. He had a daughter of own, and she has me. After many years, his story has finally been told for others to discover, and by extension his memory has been revived from the dusty pages of the past. Although it is impossible to truly recreate a person from fragments of records and hazy memories, I do hope this book has gone some way to do him justice, and that wherever he is, that he is proud of me. Having travelled on this journey to discover the truth about his life and wartime experiences, I have been drawn closer to him. In some strange way, that wish to have had one conversation alone with him, and with my grandmother has somewhat been fulfilled.

I have also reconciled my own personal struggles with the writing of this book. This last chapter especially has been a source of therapy. I believe that we are all blessed with human qualities that can help us alleviate the troubles we face in our lives, whether they be through humour, resilience, or creativity. I have been fortunate enough to be bestowed with something of the latter and feel that through writing I can express myself, and in time I can also leave some record behind of what sort of person I was, and how I felt about certain things. When that pain of being childlessness by circumstance returns, and it often does, I remind myself of all the things I have, rather than what I lack. To accept who I am and my circumstances. To do what I can to help others. I am so proud to have partnered with Variety, the Children's Charity to donate the proceeds of this book to help raise funds for disabled and disadvantaged children in the UK. What better way to counter my situation. The Ancient Greek leader Pericles said, "What you leave behind is not what is engraved in stone monuments, but what is woven into the lives of others." Perhaps how one lives their life and cares for those they love is all that can really be controlled, just as my grandfather discovered. It is that ideal that now drives me forward. To make a positive difference to the world around me. I hope that will be the legacy I shall leave.

A photograph of my grandmother and I, taken in 1980

The Author and his pet cockapoo Clementine, taken in Green Park in 2021

ACKNOWLEDGMENTS

This book could not have been written without the extensive help, support and contribution of my mother, and the approval of my wife in allowing me to share our own personal story at the close of this book.

Additional, heartfelt thanks to those who have been of great support:

India Audsley, Nicholas Horne,
Anthony Mestriner, and Rob Kraitt

Special mention to our new doggie family friends and neighbours:

Teresa and Daryll Arnold, Laura and Luke Corley,
Philippa Haslegrave and Adam Werney,
Nicky and Colin McDougal,
Rachel and Dan Pemberton, Hector Pinnington,
Aga Wierzbicka and Tim Spencer

SELECT BIBLIOGRAPHY, NOTES & RESOURCES

Other than the personal testimonial of my mother (oral and typescript), the most useful primary and secondary works consulted in the research for this book are listed below, with special mentions to the exhaustive work of Robert Bickers through China Families, as well as that of author, Paul French, whose writing I found enthralling and captivating.

- Ancestry.com (digital platform for ancestral records)
- Captives of Empire website by Greg Leck (including personal email correspondence with the Author)
- Chap magazine article 'Old Shanghai' by Paul French (December 15th, 2018)
- ChinaFamilies.net (digital platform directed by Robert Bickers, Professor of History at the University of Bristol. See also RobertBickers.net)
- 'Destination Shanghai' by Paul French (Blacksmith Books, 2018)
- 'Empire of the Sun' (book) by J.G. Ballard (Harper Perennial, 2014)
- 'Empire of the Sun' (film) directed by Steven Spielberg (Warner Bros., 1988)

- <u>Gale.com</u> (The Chinese Maritime Customs Service, 1854–1949: An Introduction by Professor Richard S. Horowitz, California State University, Northridge)
- <u>Hankoutowuhan.org</u> (Hankou to Wuhan, a multimedia project tracing historical narratives of the city of Hanku)
- Harvard University library website (Chinese Maritime Customs)
- Historic Shanghai website (Greg Leck interview)
- SOAS University of London website (Chinese Maritime Customs)
- <u>ThatsMags.com</u> article 'Shanghai: The world's longest bar' by Erik Crouch)
- University of Cambridge website (History of the Maritime Customs Service)
- Virtual Shanghai website

Notes:

It is important to recognise that I have discovered some inconsistencies with names, dates, and times referenced by my mother when retelling my grandfather's life story over the years. To that end I have used factual historical records as the basis on which to chronicle these events.

Helpful resources relating to Childlessness:

- Life Without Children (fertilitynetworkuk.org)
- Mens Health (menshealthforum.org.uk/men-without-children)
- Meriel Whale Counselling (merielwhalecounselling.co.uk/childlessness-counselling)
- The Toll of Not Being Able to Have Children (Mind.org.uk)
- WorldChildlessWeek.net

Printed in Great Britain
by Amazon

11981808R00032